Artists Through
the Ages

Vincent van Gogh

Alix Wood

WINDMILL
BOOKS
™

New York

Published in 2013 by Windmill Books, An Imprint of Rosen Publishing
29 East 21st Street, New York, NY 10010

Editor for Alix Wood Books: Eloise Macgregor
US Editor: Sara Antill
Designer: Alix Wood

Photo Credits: Cover, 1, 21 © Peter Willi - Artothek; 4 top © ARC; 7 © nga; 9 © Imagno -
Artothek; 10 © Jean-Pol Grandmont; 13 © Peter Willi - Artothek; 15 © Blauel/Gnamm
- Artothek; 17 © Peter Willi - Artothek; 19 © Christie's Images Ltd - Artothek ; 22-23 ©
Hans Hinz - Artothek; 25 © Hans Hinz - Artothek; 26-27 © Artothek; 27 top © Francisco J.
Gonzalez; 29 left © philophoto/Shutterstock; 3, 4 bottom, 8, 11, 28, 29 right © Shutterstock

Library of Congress Cataloging-in-Publication Data

Wood, Alix.
 Vincent van Gogh / by Alix Wood.
    pages cm — (Artists through the ages)
 Includes index.
 ISBN 978-1-61533-622-7 (library binding) — ISBN 978-1-61533-631-9 (pbk.) —
 ISBN 978-1-61533-632-6 (6-pack)
 1. Gogh, Vincent van, 1853–1890—Juvenile literature. 2. Painters—Netherlands—
 Biography—Juvenile literature. I. Title.
 ND653.G7W66 2013
 759.9492—dc23
 [B]
                              2012028071

Manufactured in the United States of America

CPSIA Compliance Information: Batch #BW13WM: For Further Information contact Windmill Books, New York, New York at 1-866-478-0556

Contents

Who Was Vincent van Gogh?

Vincent Willem van Gogh was born on March 30, 1853 in Groot-Zundert, a village near Breda in the Netherlands. He was the oldest child of Theodorus van Gogh, a minister of the Dutch Reformed Church, and Anna Cornelia Carbentus. Vincent was a painter well known for his bold colors and his swirly style of painting.

Vincent van Gogh

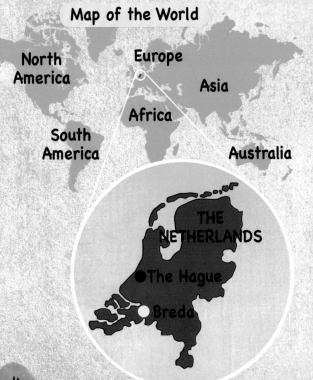

Map of the World

North America

Europe

Asia

Africa

South America

Australia

THE NETHERLANDS

●The Hague

Breda

Breda, North Brabant, the Netherlands, today

Vincent was close to his younger brother Theo. He also had another brother and three sisters. Vincent was a serious, quiet child. He went to the local village school, where one teacher taught around 200 pupils! After a year, he and his sister Anna were taught at home by a **governess**, until he went to boarding school at Zevenbergen about 20 miles (32 km) away. He was sad to leave his family. At 13 Vincent went to college, but left suddenly at 15 without graduating.

Vincent's brother, Theo

Vincent's Art

Vincent began to draw as a child, but he did not begin painting until his late twenties. Then, in just over ten years, he painted 860 oil paintings and more than 1,300 watercolors, drawings, sketches, and prints! He is best known for his **self-portraits** and his landscapes of cypress trees, wheat fields, and sunflowers.

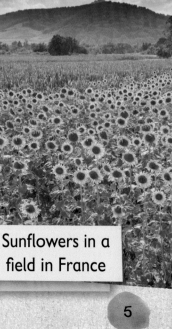

Sunflowers in a field in France

Vincent's First Jobs

Vincent's first job was working for the firm of **art dealers**, Goupil & Cie. His uncle Vincent, who he called "Uncle Cent" helped him get the job. After training in The Hague, in the Netherlands, he moved to a branch in London, England. This was a happy time for Vincent. He was successful and was, at 20, earning more than his father. Vincent then moved to the main branch in Paris, France.

Goupil & Cie, in Paris

Vincent began to dislike art being treated as a thing to buy and sell. Customers sensed his dislike, which wasn't good for business. In the end, his boss fired him. Vincent returned to England and taught at a boarding school. He then worked in a bookstore in the Netherlands for six months. Unhappy, he spent his time doodling or translating the Bible into English, French, and German.

Vincent decided to follow his father and become a **missionary**. His parents agreed to pay for his education, but Vincent started work as a minister with the coal miners of Borinage, a poor area of Belgium. He liked the miners, their lifestyles, and their families. After working there for a while, his brother Theo persuaded him to use his artistic talent and become an artist instead.

The Potato Eaters, 1885. When Vincent painted in later years, he remembered the working people of Borinage.

Letters to Theo

Vincent missed his brother Theo when he was away. The two wrote to each other often. They exchanged hundreds of letters between 1872 and 1890, with more than 600 from Vincent to Theo and 40 from Theo to Vincent. The only gap was a time when Vincent lived in Paris, because the brothers lived together and had no need to write!

Vincent sketched pictures in his letters and often wrote notes all around the edge of the paper. With so many letters going to and from Vincent's house, it's not surprising he got to know a postman very well! He was good friends with postman Joseph Roulin (right), and painted several portraits of his whole family. Vincent's letters were very interesting. In them he described what he was painting and often did little drawings of his work to show Theo what they looked like.

RÉPUBLIQUE FRANÇAISE

CARTE POSTALE

Ce côté est exclusivement réservé à l'adresse

Tél. 36-56

Portrait of Joseph Roulin, 1889

Choosing Art

Vincent moved to Cuesmes, in Belgium. His interest in being a minister began to fade. He decided to become an artist instead. Theo helped Vincent by sending money, and Vincent took some lessons at an art academy in Brussels.

The house where Van Gogh stayed in Cuesmes in 1880, when he decided to become an artist

No, Nay, Never

In the countryside near Breda, Vincent spent time walking and talking with his cousin, Kee Vos-Stricker. He asked her to marry him, but she said no. In fact, she said, "No, nay, never!" Kee's father wouldn't let Vincent see her and this upset him. That Christmas Vincent refused to go to church, argued violently with his father, and left home.

In April 1881, Vincent moved to the countryside near Breda with his family, and then later to The Hague. There, he spent time with Anton Mauve, a relative, who was a painter. Mauve lent him money to set up a **studio**. The two soon had a disagreement and stopped speaking, though.

Still restless, Vincent moved to his parent's new home in Nuenen. He liked to paint weavers at work, and his neighbor Margot Begemann sometimes went painting with him. They wanted to marry, but their families were against it. Margot tried to poison herself, and Vincent had to rush her to the hospital. At the same time, he started getting interest from Paris in his work. He also exhibited paintings in the window of a paint dealer in The Hague. For the next two years he did nearly 200 oil paintings! His **palette** was very dark, nothing like the bright paintings he is famous for.

Vincent's first paintings
used very dark colors.

Antwerp and Paris

In 1885, Vincent moved to Antwerp, Belgium. He had little money and hardly ate, spending the money Theo sent on painting materials and models. He went to the Academy of Fine Arts to study painting. He visited museums and admired the bright new painting styles, and he began to add brighter colors to his work.

Vincent moved to Paris in March 1886 to live with Theo, and studied at Fernand Cormon's studio. At Cormon's studio he met many other talented artists. His friends were Paul Signac, Emile Bernard, Henri de Toulouse-Lautrec, Camille Pissarro, John Russell, and later, Paul Gauguin.

Père Tanguy's Shop

Julien Tanguy ran an art supply shop in Paris. His happy nature and love of art made his shop popular, and he was nicknamed "père" or "father" Tanguy. He shared his food and money with struggling artists and happily exhibited their paintings. Tanguy would take paintings as payment for paints, so his shop was a colorful gallery!

13

A House in Arles

Vincent moved to Arles, in southern France. He stayed in two hotels before renting a house in the center called the Yellow House. He had a dream of starting an artist's **colony**. He made friends with American artist Dodge MacKnight and Danish artist Christian Mourier-Petersen. Vincent painted some of his best works in Arles. He was very busy.

This is what he painted in one month, September 1888:

The Café Terrace at Night
The Entrance to the Public Park in Arles
The Green Vineyard
A Lane in the Public Garden at Arles
Night Café in the Place Lamartine in Arles
The Old Mill
Ploughed Field
Portrait of Eugène Boch
The Poet's Garden
The Self-Portrait (Dedicated to Paul Gauguin)
The Sower: Outskirts of Arles in the Background
Starry Night Over the Rhone
Vincent's House in Arles (The Yellow House)
Portrait of Milliet, Second Lieutenant of the Zouaves

That's about two days per masterpiece!

Unsigned

Vincent didn't sign the *Café Terrace* painting. We know it was by him as he described it in a letter to his sister. He painted it on the spot, instead of in his studio from sketches. He had trouble telling the paints apart in the dark though! This is the first painting he did with his famous starry background.

The Café Terrace at Night, 1888

Bedroom in Arles

Vincent painted his bedroom in the Yellow House three times. The painting on the right was the third version, a small copy done for his mother and sister. On the wall on the right are the portraits of his friends Eugène Boch and Paul-Eugène Milliet from the list on page 14. The painting over the table is Vincent's *Peasant of Zundert* self-portrait. The painting above the bed is unknown. It may be by someone else or be a missing work.

Vincent doesn't seem to have many things in his bedroom. Neither of the doors are a closet. The door on the right went to the staircase, and the door to the left went to the guest room. His clothes and hat are hanging up on pegs. You can see a bowl and jug of water on the table ready for him to get washed. It looks at first like Vincent has painted the back wall wrong, but he hasn't. The room was an odd shape and had an angled back wall. Vincent often painted chairs like the ones in the painting.

Bedroom in Arles, 1889

Draw Your Bedroom

What would you put in a drawing of your bedroom? Will it look as tidy as Vincent's? We can guess from this painting that Vincent really liked his bedroom. His bed looks comfortable and he has all his favorite paintings around him.

A Visit from Gauguin

Vincent first met artist Paul Gauguin in Paris when Vincent had organized an art exhibition. After seeing the exhibit Gauguin arranged to swap one of his paintings for two of Vincent's sunflowers studies. When Gauguin agreed to visit Arles, Vincent hoped he would stay and help create his dream of an artist's colony.

Paul Gauguin

Vincent was very excited. He painted sunflowers to decorate Gauguin's room. Gauguin finally arrived and for two months the two lived and painted together. They visited galleries together, and Gauguin painted Vincent's portrait. After a while, their friendship began to turn sour. Vincent admired Gauguin and wanted to be treated as his equal, but Gauguin was **arrogant**. They argued a lot about art.

Fourteen Sunflowers in a Vase, 1889

The Argument and the Ear

One evening Vincent and Gauguin had an argument. Gauguin claimed Vincent threatened him with a knife. It has long been believed that later that evening Vincent went home and cut off a good part of his left ear. He then wrapped the ear in cloth and gave it as a present to a woman he knew. The police were called and Vincent was taken to the hospital.

Did Gauguin Do It?

Some think Vincent made up the story to protect Gauguin, who actually cut Vincent's ear off during the argument. Both men kept silent, Gauguin to avoid arrest and Vincent in an attempt to keep his valued friend. Gauguin was an excellent swordsman. He wanted to leave Arles, and perhaps walked out of the house with his cases and sword in his hand, but was followed by the upset Vincent. It is possible they fought, and Gauguin cut off Vincent's left earlobe, either in anger or self-defense.

Self-portrait, 1889. This was painted not long after Vincent cut off his left ear. Why can you see his left ear in this picture? Vincent painted self-portraits by looking in a mirror, so this is really his right ear.

21

The Asylum

Vincent returned home but spent the next month going back and forth to the hospital suffering from **hallucinations** and thinking he was being poisoned. In March, 30 people from Arles wrote to ask the police to close Vincent's house so he couldn't return. They called him the "fou roux," or "the redheaded madman."

By May, still struggling with his mental health, Vincent decided to go into an **asylum**. Vincent was thought to have a type of epilepsy. The asylum was surrounded by cornfields, vineyards, and olive trees. Theo arranged for two cells next to each other for Vincent, so that one could be used as a studio. As long as he remained stable, the doctors let Vincent paint. He did 150 paintings during his stay.

The Hospital at Arles, 1889. Vincent was stopped from painting after he tried to eat his paint during one attack. After a while, the doctors let him paint again.

The Starry Night

The Starry Night is probably Vincent van Gogh's best known painting. The painting is of the view outside his window at the asylum. Unusual for Vincent, it was painted from memory during the day. Perhaps that is how he got so much feeling into the painting.

Vincent used thick brush strokes and often used paint straight out of the tube. He laid down each stroke of color carefully and separately. His style was influenced by an **Impressionist** style called *pointillism* where dots of primary colors are put on the canvas and our eyes mix them to create other colors. Vincent used strokes instead, using the direction, length, and curve to get the look he wanted. The twirling sky is full of curving and short brush strokes while the still, peaceful buildings have straight, longer lines.

Here is an example of how pointillism works. Only dots of the three primary colors, red, blue, and yellow, have been used. Where the dots of yellow and blue are close to each other, your eyes mix the color so it looks green.

The Starry Night, 1889

Happy or Sad Painting?

What do you think? The village is dark and the swirly clouds in the night sky could seem frightening. The brightly lit windows in the village make it look homely and friendly, though, and the church in the middle might be protecting the houses.

Vincent's Last Days

When Vincent left the asylum he moved to Auvers-sur-Oise, near Paris, to be close to his doctor and to Theo. During the two months between his arrival, on May 21, and his death on July 29, Vincent did about seventy paintings. That's more than one a day!

On July 27, Vincent shot himself in the chest with a revolver. Where he was when he shot himself is unclear, perhaps the wheatfield or at a barn near the inn where he was staying. He managed to get back to the inn, the Auberge Ravoux, and two doctors were called. They couldn't remove the bullet. The following morning Theo rushed to be with Vincent. At first it seemed as if he would get better, but he died in the evening of infection in the wound.

Vincent died in a room on the top floor of the Auberge Ravoux (right), where he had been staying. When asked if he had meant to kill himself, he apparently replied "Yes I believe so." Some think he was shot by a teenage boy who used to buy him drinks and tease him. His easel and brushes that he had taken to the fields with him that day were never found, and neither was a suicide note or gun.

Wheatfield with Crows, 1890.
This was one of Vincent's last paintings.

Vincent's Legacy

A legacy is what is left behind when someone dies. Usually it is money, or things that the person owned, to be inherited by their children. Vincent wrote in a letter to Theo that, as he did not have any children, he saw his paintings as his children.

Van Gogh's new approach to painting had a strong influence on the next generation of artists. His use of unusual colors, the angular heavy line, his obvious brushstrokes and patterns, and his **distortion** of reality all influenced many artists who followed.

Vincent's Grave

Vincent was buried the day after he died in the cemetery behind the church at Auvers-sur-Oise. Theo died the following year from a mixture of illness and grief at the loss of his brother. The two were eventually buried side by side.

ICI REPOSE
VINCENT van GOGH
1853 1890

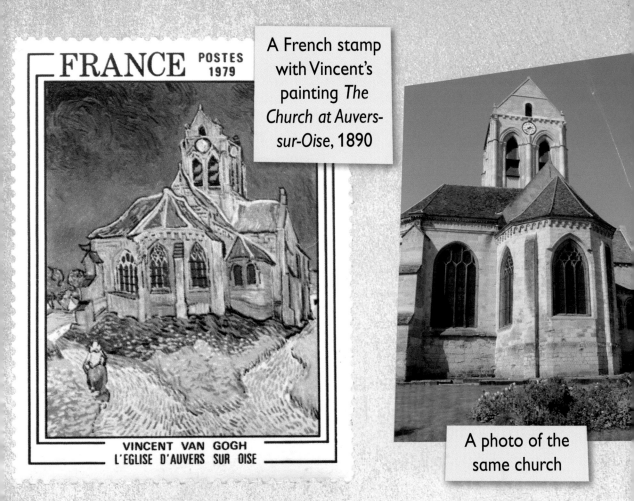

FRANCE POSTES 1979

VINCENT VAN GOGH
L'EGLISE D'AUVERS SUR OISE

A French stamp with Vincent's painting *The Church at Auvers-sur-Oise*, 1890

A photo of the same church

The church in the painting and in the photograph above are clearly the same building. The difference is the painting gives the church a character and atmosphere that the photo does not. That is what Vincent made his paintings do. In another letter to Theo, Vincent said "real painters do not paint things as they are. They paint them as they themselves feel them to be." That ability is Vincent's legacy that he leaves behind for us all.

Glossary

arrogant
(AHR-uh-gant)
Overly proud of oneself or one's own opinions.

art dealers
(ART DEE-lurz)
People or companies that buy and sell works of art.

asylum (uh-SY-lum)
An institution for the care of those unable to care for themselves and especially for the insane.

colony (KAH-luh-nee)
A group of people with common interests who live close to each other.

distortion
(dih-STAWR-shun)
The condition of being twisted out of a natural or original shape.

governess
(GUH-vur-nes)
A woman who teaches and trains a child in a private home.

hallucinations
(huh-loo-sih-NAY-shunz)
Seeing things that are not
really there.

Impressionist
(im-PREH-shuh-nist)
An artist who
concentrates on the
impression of a scene
using unmixed primary
colors and small brush
strokes to simulate light.

missionary
(MIH-shuh-ner-ee)
A person spreading

religious faith among
unbelievers or engaging
in charitable work with
religious support.

palette (PA-lit)
A board used by a painter
to mix paints on.

self-portraits
(self-POR-tretz)
Paintings of oneself made
by oneself.

studio (STOO-dee-oh)
The working place of
an artist.

Websites

For web resources related to the
subject of this book, go to:
www.windmillbooks.com/weblinks
and select this book's title.

Read More

Green, Jen. *Vincent van Gogh*. Artists in Their Time. Danbury, CT: Franklin Watts, 2002.

Nichols, Catherine. *Vincent van Gogh*. The Primary Source Library of Famous Artists. New York: PowerKids Press, 2006.

Van Gogh, Vincent, and The Metropolitan Museum of Art. *Vincent's Colors*. San Francisco, CA: Chronicle Books, 2005.

Index